BREAKING

THE

STRONGHOLD

OF

SPIRIT

SPOUSES

Nykefah Nairne

Unless otherwise stated, all scriptures are quoted from the King James Version, New King James Version, Amplified Version, or Complete Jewish Bible.

ISBN: 9798531320100

Independently published

Copyright 2021 by Nykefah Nairne

Publishing, Editing by ParaFount.

St. Catherine, Jamaica

More Popular Books by Nykefah Nairne

- The Wife in Transit
- Breaking the Stronghold of Spirit Spouses
- Breaking the Mental Stronghold of Spirit Spouses
- Breaking the Financial Stronghold of Spirit Spouses
- Breaking the Stronghold of Gossip
- Breaking the Stronghold of Deceit

DEDICATION

I'd especially like to dedicate this book to singles stuck in a cycle of dysfunctional, unfruitful, and stagnant relationships, which usually lead back to singleness. This book reveals that your relational struggles, the delayed or hindered marriage period, the abrupt breakups, or engagement break-offs were not your fault but the enemy's work. I pray that you will continue to believe God for marriage, understand what is fighting against you, and receive complete deliverance through revelation and the power of Jesus.

Nykefah Nairne

TABLE OF CONTENTS

INTRODUCTION

If you understand the concept of sin, you'll know that we live in a fallen world. We live in a world filled with humans but with spiritual entities at work in a realm that is typically "unseen" unless revealed or encountered. With that being the case, there are often instances where both worlds collide, or the activities taking place in one realm are immediately felt and perceived in the other. In this book, we will look into the realities of sexually immoral spiritual entities or powers that disturbingly interfere with the lives & relationships of humans in the natural realm.

As Believers, we must understand that we are very much spiritual beings. Living in a mortal, time-bound body does not negate the reality of the unseen, spiritual realm beyond our earthly mind's comprehension; it is still a part of our reality as citizens of the kingdom of God. It is argued that spiritual things, some not explicitly outlined in the Bible, are not real, not recorded, and are therefore totally nonexistent.

Nykefah Nairne

However, just because something isn't explicitly addressed, mentioned, or outlined the way we want it to be in scripture doesn't mean the spiritual reality and power of them aren't actual. There are many gods and idols mentioned in the Bible whose demonic powers are still at work in the lives and generations of people today.

Though spirit spouses' names, assignments and powers may not always be mentioned in scripture, it doesn't cancel the continuance of their demonic agendas. One of the spiritual forces at work that are controversial in the ministry of deliverance and the lives of Believers is spirit spouses. These are sexually immoral spiritual beings, whether "spirit husband" or "spirit wife", that spiritually wed and attached themselves to humans and claimed them as their own, whether through doors of sin or curses.

These demonic spirits are most commonly known as "Incubus" (male) and "Succubus" (female). They usually appear and enter spiritually through dreams or manifest naturally to come upon their victims while they sleep to sexually assault them (rape, molestation, etc.). They are the reasons people have consistent, perverse and uncontrollable sexual/"wet dreams" while they sleep.

They come with many "side-effects" and wreak havoc on a much larger scale beyond what many can comprehend or wish to accept. Once they enter through a dream, which is any dream that involves sex/sexual activities with anything or anyone or a questionable/strange wedding ceremony, they now begin to operate in your life.

You'll then begin to experience the signs and other things listed in this book that result from their presence. Though they are not openly identified in scripture, they are very much at work spiritually. Knowing that there is nothing new under the sun, neither spiritually nor physically, means these demonic spirits have been around long before.

Ephesians 6, verses 11 and 12, is a somewhat broad yet profoundly distinct scripture on the realities of various spiritual entities at work on the earth. The rest speaks about putting on the whole armour of God. There would be no need for armour if there weren't known and unknown forces to be warring against, whether or not they're specifically mentioned.

As the Apostle Paul writes in verse 11, we can see the need for the ultimate armour of God that will be able to help Believers withstand the wiles ("devious or cunning stratagems employed in manipulating or persuading someone to do what one wants") of the devil. And, as for verse 12, which says, "For we are not struggling against human beings, but against the rulers, authorities and cosmic powers governing this darkness, against the spiritual forces of evil in the heavenly realm", it tells us that the warfare we face as Believers is not one against people or humans, but against spiritual forces.

They are not just miniature spiritual forces but literal rulers, authorities, and cosmic powers that govern darkness and against spiritual evil within the heavenly realm. That being said, even without mentioning "spirit spouses" or any other spirits today that manifest through people during deliverance, it is noticeably clear that there are spiritual forces at work, though not mentioned or outlined, but are as real as the natural forces of evil in our natural realm and understanding.

Spiritual spouses (spirits that illegally marry, sexually assault, and hold hostage the lives of humans) are as real as natural spouses. They appear in dreams through familiar or unknown faces and continue to visit their victims in like manner through whoever they wish to appear as. These spirits have an assignment to wed/tie/join themselves to the lives of humans, which in return hinders or completely blocks the person from marrying a natural, earthly spouse or maintaining any godly intimate relationship by whatever means.

This book teaches more about the nature of these spirits, how they enter and operate, and how to overcome their grips with the power of our Lord Jesus Christ!

Nykefah Nairne

THE AGENDA OF SPIRIT SPOUSES

Spirit spouses (spirit husband/spirit wife) are relentless, sexually perverted demons that attach themselves to the lives of humans through sexual immorality, witchcraft, and curses. The nature of their attacks opens the door for a "spiritual marriage" where they join themselves to their victims, most commonly through sexual dreams or even enticing gifts. They do this with the intent of becoming one with them, to kill further, steal, and destroy their life and destiny.

Spirit spouses affect the lives of those they're attached to in various ways through this spiritual act of marriage. They can and will affect their finances, progress, spiritual growth, purity, success, relationships, marriages, and souls at large (mind, will, and emotions). With all these, spirit spouses often work alongside spirits of frustration, anger, rage, disappointment, and failure to carry out their plans to the greatest extent.

When it comes to a person's progress, spirit spouses, because of their jealous and possessive nature, hinder the person from progressing to keep them to themselves and at one place in life. If the person's progress is to come through a genuine blessing and not from the enemy's deceit, the spirit will do all it can to stop this person's progress, promotion, or acceleration.

Financially, they cause a lack or completely block finances from locating you by means of anybody else blessing you or favouring you. They will even block the finances of your partner to cause relational frustration between the two. It will become hard for you to have abundance financially or receive particular levels of financial breakthroughs and outpourings.

They will even make it hard for you to keep money. In contrast, you will get it but not be able to save it or will not necessarily "see" where it went or what it was spent on. If you're to be promoted in any way, whether naturally or spiritually, these spirits will make it their duty to hinder or completely stop it from happening. Naturally, they will put people in a place or demonically orchestrate events that do not occur in your favour.

They will set people against you, and when your promotion is to happen, suddenly or eventually, it will pass you, be given elsewhere, be dormant, get held up, or will no longer be in place to happen. These spirits want you to remain at whatever level you are at with them, wanting no one and nothing to break you from their hold and influence. Spiritually, they hinder your promotion in the spirit (spiritual growth and authority) by affecting you through sexual impurity, which affects your mind.

They know you should have a mind renewed in Christ, fervency, consistency, and intimacy in your prayer life, purity and worship, and a dedicated fasting life. These spirits understand the need for Believers to grow spiritually, remain in purity, and stay holy and undefiled.

So, they do what they can to defile Believers or to let them believe that they are too unclean for God and to be involved in anything that has to do with service unto God. In their agenda is the need to sexually defile you, causing you to feel unclean, shameful, guilty, and condemned so that you stay away from praying, fasting, worshipping, reading, or having any private/public service unto God.

Another way in which they spiritually afflict Believers is to defile them through their sexual acts and to defile their minds especially. Through sexual encounters, they cause Believers to be impure even in thoughts and sometimes actions. They breed lust in the hearts and minds of those they afflict. Hence, persons under the influence or affliction of the spirit spouse can find themselves being uncontrollably lustful in thought.

They have sexual thoughts that even they hate to have and urges they cannot always comprehend. Additionally, though they are sexually immoral spirits, they can be considered as a stronghold/strongman. This often makes it hard for some persons to be delivered from them. They set up holds in the minds of their victims and control their thoughts, actions, decisions, and even their moods.

They not only remain sexually attached, but they now have somewhat cemented themselves in the mind (thoughts) of whoever they're afflicting. Success, for spirit spouses, must come only through them and the compromise of the kingdom of darkness.

If you're working hard but not seeing rewards or goals met, encountering many failures, disappointments, and delays, it could be the work of spirit spouses. With them being a part of your life, though you will work hard by integral and godly means, they will try to hinder your success because they want to be the source of it. And, if you continue to serve God in your work, they will do their best to oppose the rewards of your work.

Now, as it relates to relationships and marriages, these spirits hit people hard! They despise a man and a woman in Christ, coming together as one. They hate marriage, just like the Adversary who sent them. They hate unions, and they will try anything to keep relationships and marriages from happening or prospering.

They make it their duty for couples to argue (especially without a clear cause), to have serious miscommunication or lack of communication, loss of interest in each other, frustration at the other partner, financial hardships, love growing cold, mood swings toward each other, stagnancy, and hindrance of an engagement or marriage in general.

These spirits afflict marriage and relationships in the lives of people. They cause relational strife, contention, confusion, and a lack of peace, leaving either or both partners questioning God's will for their relationship. But the truth is, Satan doesn't war against or oppose himself or his agenda. He will only try to sever, frustrate, and hinder what God is doing.

Overall, their agenda, like their master Satan, is to kill, steal, and destroy the lives, destinies, and souls of human beings to drive them away from God and His purpose for their lives. These spirits are brutal in their attacks and possessiveness. They will frustrate your life, walk with God, relationships, marriages, and all they can to keep you in their grips.

HOW SPIRIT SPOUSES ENTER

Like many other spiritual entities that enter a natural body or an individual's life, spirit spouses enter through dreams, sin, demonic altars, or witchcraft curses. Naturally, before accepting Christ, we must understand that we were born in sin and live in a fallen world. We were born in a world where the unseen, supernatural realm is active, and there are always spirits looking for earthly hosts to carry out the enemy's agenda.

Naturally, they do this by entering the lives and bodies of persons and setting up a stronghold to exert a particular level of control. On the matter of sin, which is the most apparent open door, spirit spouses will enter a person's life and affect everything they do. Now, the goal of sin is to separate us from God. The wages (rewards) of sin are death, and that can be spiritual death while here on earth, which leads to ultimate death on earth and after earth (complete separation from God, His light, and the Kingdom of Heaven).

When we sin, we open the door for this spirit to become a host. You might say, "But I have repented of my sins, believed in Christ, and am now living for Him," and that is true, yes. He loves you, has accepted you, and you are now living for him, but there is still an undealt with strongholds. You are forgiven; however, there can still be a need for deliverance and the continued process of salvation to do a work in you.

And, if deliverance is still needed for God's children, it means there is still work to do in their lives if the complete manifestation of His Spirit and Presence isn't evident. So, do not be discouraged or even prideful to think you are far from having a spiritual strongman or any spirit afflicting your life. Now, spirit spouses can enter through sexual sin. Here are several ways they can attach themselves to you:

1. **Fornication**
2. **Sexual Assault (Rape, Molestation, Fondling, etc.)**
3. **Adultery (this can cause an even greater curse on your life beyond just spirit spouses)**
4. **The spirit of lust (can be transferred, invited, or can enter through lustful or seductive "entertainment")**

5. **Pornography (watching it, whether "hardcore" or through "mild" means such as movies, TV shows, etc.)**

6. **Masturbation**

7. **Homosexuality**

8. **Any other form of Sexual Perversion**

Therefore, if you have ever participated in any of these sexual acts or been a victim of any, there may be a strong possibility that a spirit spouse has attached themselves to you and has/had a legal right to be in your life. Curses and witchcraft are two other popular ways these spirits attach themselves to persons.

They can come through generational/bloodline curses that have not been addressed and stopped, spoken/word curses where people speak against a person's relationship, relational progress, or marriage in general ("he/she shouldn't/will never get married", "I hope their relationship doesn't work out", etc.).

Or, the curses can be any form of verbal or communicated hatred against a person in the area of love that manifests as a spirit spouse and makes way for them (opens the door) to be assigned to a person's life, relationship, or marriage. Curses in this area can merely be anyone speaking against God's will, goodness, peace, and joy for your life relationally or maritally.

You may wonder why or how anyone could curse you or if it would even be accurate, but you would be surprised how many persons, through envy, insecurity, jealousy, and hatred, are against this area of your life. Some may even believe that you are undeserving and unworthy of love, peace, and the goodness of God.

Witchcraft (manipulation) is not new to the earth and has affected marriages for centuries (ask Adam and Eve). Witchcraft, according to Wikipedia, is "the practice of what the practitioner ("witch") believes to be *supernatural* skills and abilities, such as the casting of *spells* and the performance of magical *rituals*... historically, the most common meaning is the use of *supernatural* means to cause harm to the innocent;".

Through witchcraft, more practically, some persons involve themselves in casting spells, practising voodoo, obeah, speaking incantations, and setting up demonic altars against people and families to afflict them in the area of marriage. They will not only utter curses, but some will go as far as to use even objects, pictures, and personal items from or of the individual they wish to curse as points of contact to perform their works.

These spells can hinder, delay, and frustrate someone who desires marriage, is in a relationship, is about to be engaged, or is already married. Another way these spirits enter is through demonically erected altars in a person's bloodline. Every family and individual's life has good and bad altars at work.

according to the Miriam-Webster dictionary, an altar is "a usually raised structure or place on which sacrifices are offered or incense is burned in worship; often used figuratively to describe a thing given great or undue precedence or value, especially at the cost of something else. (e.g., sacrificed his family life on the altar of career advancement)".

An altar could have been erected in your family or against your family and is working against relationships and marriages now affecting you. These altars are places set up to ensure that spirits are assigned to you and carry out the enemy's work in your life. Unless these altars and their works are addressed and broken in the name and power of Jesus Christ, they will continue to wreak havoc and fulfil their assignments.

Altars can be set up by anybody, anywhere, and do not need to be geographically close to you to work against you. You can live in one country or region of the world and have an altar working against you in that same country or region or completely different ones. Altars, the reality of witchcraft, and the reality and works of curses against nations and people can all be found and proven in the scriptures.

When it comes to our dreams, they are one of the ways God speaks to us. Things that are naturally and spiritually hidden are now revealed. Through dreams, we have access to spiritual revelations we are unaware of while awake. Before anything manifests naturally, it must occur spiritually, and dreams are one of the ways these things are highlighted to us. Based on the nature of spirit spouses, it is easy to spot them in dreams. They usually come in the form of the opposite sex. Their faces can either be hidden or unknown, or they can take on a familiar face and come as that person in your dreams. They come with the general intention of sex and perversion.

They often enter through sexual activities in dreams where they will have sex with you in a dream. Still, it is signifying them having sex with you spiritually and sometimes even naturally. They can also enter through dreams of marriage/marrying a stranger or familiar face who is not your wife/wife-to-be/husband/husband-to-be (natural partner).

In this way, they wed themselves to you spiritually, which hinders anyone from naturally committing to you. Even if they do, the spirits will try to cause separation.

SIGNS, CHARACTERISTICS & OPERATIONS OF SPIRIT SPOUSES

Like any other living entity, these spirits have distinct characteristics and traits that help them to be recognized at work. They operate in various ways, but always with the overarching agenda of the devil – to kill, steal, and ultimately destroy the lives of whoever they are attached to. With these signs and traits, you can identify them in your life after they have entered through dreams, witchcraft, curses, or sins. This means they operate through you, and these traits will reflect through you, your life, and the things that happen to and around you. Here are some traits, signs they exhibit, and the operations they carry out:

1. They are jealous/possessive.

With this trait, deliverance can sometimes be difficult as they are very jealous of their host, want nobody else to have them, and will often refuse to let them go easily. They believe that the person's body and life belong to them, and hence, they become very possessive of them.

Relationally, they exhibit this nature by causing you to be indifferent toward your partner and, by all means, try to separate you from your partner or to keep them at bay. They hate the idea of 2 partners being close, affectionate, and intimate with each other and will, therefore, in their jealous and possessive ways, do things to cause separation, loss of interest, etc., to keep their host to themselves.

They will affect your mood, thoughts, behaviours, speech, and overall actions to turn away or ward off your natural partner to keep you to yourself.

2. They are extremely lustful and erotic.

They mostly come via dreams and visions at night, as strangers or familiar faces. They carry with them a heavy spirit of lust, which may or may not be uncontrollable but can also be unexplainable and 'random'. They are very erotic (sexually explicit) in their behaviours and actions towards you or just through projections within the mind. They are very sexually unclean/filthy. They desire to web their prey in constant thoughts, desires, feelings, and dreams that include anything lustful, sexual, and abnormal.

These thoughts, feelings, and the results of their actions towards you can cause shame, guilt, and condemnation. They can also attack you while awake, which happens in more extreme cases of constantly feeling lustful or as if you're engaging in sexual activities even while you're wide awake when physically you're doing no such thing.

3. They are aggressive and remorseless.

In attacking you at night, they are incredibly aggressive and have no remorse for the effects of their actions on you. They are sexually ruthless and will do with you as they please, by whatever means. Even in deliverance, they usually display violence and aggression in refusing to let their hosts go and will put up a fight.

4. They are determined and persistent.

These spirits are neither weak nor timid but resilient and bold in their agenda and must carry it out. They are determined to fulfil whatever duty they have in their life and persist in showing up accordingly. They will make it clear to you that they don't intend to leave and will put up a fight if you do try to remove them and their holds from your life.

They persistently show up, sometimes even at their appointed or preferred times (late night or early morning hours, or sometimes during the day).

5. They weaken your prayer life and service to God.

When they show up in your dreams, they affect your prayer life and personal service to God. Feelings of uncleanness, shame, guilt, condemnation, and the lustful aura they bring keep you from approaching or talking to God as you ought to. In this way, they hinder you from growing in prayer because you'll believe that you're too dirty to go to God for repentance, cleansing, or any form of restoration. They assault you, leaving you feeling how you're feeling, and you will begin to pray less, worship less, and seek God less, and your spiritual growth will ultimately be hindered or slowed down.

6. They will make you resentful of your spouse/potential spouse/the opposite sex in general.

Naturally, you'd adore your partner and be affectionate to them. However, with the presence of spirit spouses, you may find yourself sometimes nonchalant or hostile towards your partner or the opposite sex in unexplainable moodiness.

7. They cause constant arguments, contention, and a lack of peace in relationships/marriages.

And when you look back, these arguments had no real issues at the root except for the work of the spirit spouse. They will cause arguments and stir up constant strife between you, your partner/the opposite sex.

8. They cause misfortune and loss.

Not just relationally but financially and otherwise.

9. **They cause relational/marital confusion.**

10. **They cause strange and stubborn illnesses and diseases.**

11. They cause diseases and illnesses that have to do with the womb (endometriosis, BV, cysts, vaginal infections, STIs, STDs, etc.).

12. They cause you to be unexplainably moody and irritable towards your partner.

13. They interfere with your personal and relational joy, peace, and purpose.

14. They love giving gifts (natural means of enticement – they can also enter your life in this way through people giving you tainted gifts)

15. They can come through demonic/ungodly/evil associations.

16. They cause cycles of failed relationships, heartbreak, the opposite sex suddenly/unexpectedly losing interest in you, ghosting you/abandoning you.

17. They cause late marriage or delay/hinder marriage altogether.

18. They cause one to decide, out of frustration, to remain single when God desires for that person to marry.

19. They will cause constant sexual or lustful dreams and feelings (having sex with you in your dreams).
20. They cause miscarriages.
21. They cause barrenness in women & low sperm count in men.

Additional signs of their presence in a person's life:

1. When you miss your menstrual cycle in a dream.
2. The physical disappearance of/dreams of your marriage ring missing.
3. Sudden/unexpected loss of jobs and valuables just after your natural marriage ceremony.
4. When your loving spouse suddenly becomes your enemy.
5. When one is unexplainably pregnant in a dream. (depending on the context)
6. Breastfeeding in a dream (context matters) and even seeing one's breast secreting milk physically.
7. Inability to naturally conceive.

8. Having unusual and unexplainable body odors and vaginal infections, knowing your general and natural health are alright.

9. Constant wet dreams.

10. Having an unexplainable wedding in your dreams, especially to a stranger.

11. Nursing children in a dream. (context matters).

12. Inability to maintain a holy and pure life.

13. When one is suddenly/unexpected/constantly always jilted (rejected or abandoned) by a serious partner/partners/potential partner.

14. Feeling unexplainably tired every morning upon waking up.

HOW TO OVERCOME & DEFEAT SPIRIT SPOUSES

Though the works and afflictions of these spirits are real and powerful, their powers are no match for the name, power, and blood of Jesus Christ of Nazareth. However, to defeat a thing, we must first acknowledge its reality, existence, and tactics and then confront it. Spirit Spouses are spiritual strongmen. Strongmen are not easily moved, hence their name, but they can be moved, and that's enough to be confident about. To be delivered from it, you must come to a place of confessing that it is real, and it is operating in your life at some level.

This makes it easier to manifest, confess its assignment, and even be cast out of your life for good. To deny its existence is to deny your deliverance and the power of God. And, though everyone's deliverance experience is different, a number of things can still be applied for your own deliverance to take place. You can go through self-deliverance or have a deliverance minister cast the spirit out of you.

The methods below can be applied personally or with help from a deliverance minister or anyone God will lead to help deliver you. This person does not have to be your leader, as not all leaders believe in, understand, or operate in the ministry of deliverance, sadly. However, pray for the leading of the Holy Spirit to either help you through self-deliverance or lead you to a godly person or ministry where it can be done.

Before doing anything else, the first three things to note or "apply" to your deliverance process are these:

1. Acknowledge the existence of spirit husband/wife in your life.

This makes deliverance (especially self-deliverance) easier because what is not accepted or confessed will remain hidden and stubborn, refusing to manifest or come out. Know that acknowledging their presence and signs is not coming into agreement with them.

2. Accept Jesus Christ as your Lord and Savior.

No spirit, strongman, or evil power within this earth can be eradicated entirely without Christ.

The belief in Christ Jesus, his name, his power, and the acceptance of him as Lord enables a person to receive, keep and maintain true deliverance from evil. Upon accepting Jesus Christ into your life and being saved, you now have access to the power of his name, his blood, and the hosts of heaven to work on your behalf.

You can now use the Word of God as your sword and adequately apply warfare strategies (prayer, fasting, worship, word) to overcome this strongman. Accepting Jesus Christ is as easy as believing in his name and confessing this belief with your mouth. If you have not yet accepted Christ or you're a backslider and you desire to recommit your life to him to be delivered, here is how:

Romans 10:9-10: "Because if you acknowledge and confess with your mouth that Jesus is Lord [recognizing His power, authority, and majesty as God], and believe in your heart that God raised Him from the dead, you will be saved. For with the heart a person believes [in Christ as Savior] resulting in his justification [that is, being made righteous — being freed of the guilt of sin and made acceptable to God]; and with the mouth he acknowledges and confesses [his faith openly], resulting in and confirming [his] salvation."

Nykefah Nairne

Now it's time to put in some work to get yourself delivered! Here are the basic steps:

3. Repent of your sins (personal and generational).

You've believed in and accepted Christ, and now you are a part of the kingdom of God. Though you've accepted Christ and are now saved and baptized (ensure to do a water baptism; it holds significance), you are still expected to repent and live a repentant life. Accepting Him makes you free from the wages of sins, etc.. However, it is still essential to identify the sins you or your ancestors have committed knowingly or unknowingly and to repent of them (confess them, turn your mind away from them entirely and live a life surrendered to the standard of God). This helps in deliverance as it lets the spirit spouse blatantly know that you are no longer a slave to their control, you've denounced their influence and stronghold, and that you're committing to Christ.

The act of repentance in the heart, mind, and orally is a statement of removing yourself from past sins and coming into a renewed mental and spiritual state where the only spirit having dominion over your life is the Holy Spirit.

These specific repentance prayers are designed to confess your sins and openly acknowledge the sins of those who were before you in your family. Often, spirit spouses can be generational, whereas no one in the bloodline has ever repented of them; hence, they continue to operate through that door of iniquity.

Prayer of Repentance

Heavenly Father,

Thank you for saving me. I thank you for first loving me and accepting me into your kingdom of light. Thank you for the blessing and inheritance of Christ Jesus which now enables me to obtain deliverance and life more abundantly in you. Thank you for access to deliverance, which is my portion. I am grateful that you desire to set my life free and that you have begun a good work of deliverance in me.

Today, I confess my sins before you, both the known and unknown ones. I confess even the sins of my ancestors and all those in my bloodline who never surrendered to Christ or your will.

I ask that you forgive us for sinning against you (openly mention the sins). Forgive us for allowing this spiritual strongman (spirit husband/wife) to reign in our lives and our relational affairs. I pray that you will forgive us of this iniquity and close the door of any such related sin in my life and bloodline from this day onwards.

I receive your forgiveness and I denounce the works, influence, power, and stronghold of the spirit spouse and all other spirits it comes with. Lord, take your rightful place on the throne of my heart. Take your rightful place in my mind, body, spirit, and soul. Remove these spirits and their holds from my life through my repentance, and set me free, in the name of Jesus Christ. Amen.

PRAYERS OF RENUNCIATION OF SPIRIT SPOUSES

To "Renounce" means to reject. And in this deliverance process, you must reject this spirit spouse, its works and all that comes with it! Let's pray!

Heavenly Father,
I thank you for the power and authority to renounce things and spirits from my life that are not of you. I thank you that your plans for my life, my destiny, my relationship/marriage are good and that you mean me well. I renounce this spirit spouse and all that it comes with. I pray that all ties with this spirit in my life will be broken in the name of Jesus and it shall be completely removed from me!

Prayer Points Continued:

➢ Spirit husband/wife, I command you to release me now by fire, in the name of Jesus!
➢ Every spirit husband/wife, I divorce you by the blood of Jesus!

- Every spirit wife/spirit husband, die now, in the name of Jesus!
- Everything you have deposited in my life, come out now by fire, in the name of Jesus!
- Every power that is working against my marriage, my life, my destiny, fall down and die, in the name of Jesus!
- I divorce and renounce my marriage with the spirit husband or wife, in the name of Jesus.
- I renounce all covenants entered into with the spirit husband or wife, in the name of Jesus!
- I command the fire of God to burn to ashes the wedding gown, ring, photographs, and all other materials used for the marriage, in Jesus' name!
- I send the fire of God to burn to ashes any related marriage certificate, in the name of Jesus!
- I break every blood and soul-tie covenants with the spirit husband or wife, in the name of Jesus!
- I send the fire of God to burn to ashes any children born to this spiritual marriage, in Jesus' name!

➢ I withdraw my blood, body fluid/sperm and any other part of my body deposited on the altar of the spirit husband or wife, in Jesus' name!

➢ You spirit husband or wife tormenting my life and earthly relationship/marriage, I bind you with hot chains and fetters of God and cast you out of my life into the deep pit, and I command you not to ever come into my life again, in the name of Jesus!

➢ I return to you, every property of yours in my possession in the spirit world, including the dowry and whatsoever was used for the marriage and covenants, in the name of Jesus!

➢ I drain myself of all evil materials deposited in my body as a result of our sexual relation, in Jesus' name!

➢ Lord, send Holy Ghost fire into my roots and burn out all unclean things deposited in it by the spirit husband or wife, in the name of Jesus!

➢ I crush the head of any snake, deposited into my body by the spirit husband or wife to do me harm, and command it to come out, in the name of Jesus!

- I purge out, with the blood of Jesus, every evil material deposited in my womb to prevent me from having children on earth!
- Lord, repair and restore every damage done to any part of my body and my earthly relationship/marriage by the spirit husband or wife, in the name of Jesus.
- I reject and cancel every curse, evil pronouncement, spell, jinx, enchantment, and incantation placed upon me by any spirit husband/wife, in the name of Jesus!
- Every spirit spouse afflicting my life, leave my life now by fire!
- You spirit of failure and delay that comes with the spirit spouse leave my life now by fire!
- Every spirit of frustration and any spirit trying to stop good things in my life, leave my life now by fire!
- Every spirit of limitation affecting my life and progress, naturally, spiritually, and relationally, leave my life now by fire!
- I take back and possess all my earthly belongings in the custody of the spirit husband or wife, in Jesus' name!

- ➤ I command the spirit husband or wife to turn his or her back on me forever, in Jesus' name!
- ➤ I renounce any name given to me by the spirit husband or wife, in the name of Jesus!
- ➤ I cancel any evil mark or writings placed on me by any spirit spouse, in Jesus' name!
- ➤ I set myself free from the stronghold, domineering power, and bondage of the spirit husband/wife, in the name of Jesus!
- ➤ I paralyze the remote-control power and work used to destabilize my earthly relationship/marriage and to hinder me from bearing children for my earthly husband or wife, in the name of Jesus!
- ➤ Every trademark of any demonic marriage, be shaken out of my life, in the name of Jesus!
- ➤ Every evil writing, engraved by iron pens, be wiped off by the blood of Jesus!
- ➤ I declare the fire of God upon any spirit spouse that does not want to go, in the name of Jesus!
- ➤ I bring the blood of Jesus on every evidence that can be tendered by wicked spirits against me!

- I file a counter-report in the heavens against every evil marriage, in the name of Jesus!
- I refuse to supply any evidence that the enemy may use against me, in the name of Jesus!
- Let satanic exhibitions be destroyed by the blood of Jesus!
- I declare to you spirit wife/husband that there is no vacancy for you in my life!
- Spirit husband/Spirit wife your time in my life has now come to an end! ENOUGH IS ENOUGH! IT IS FINISHED! in the name of Jesus Christ of Nazareth!

Some altered prayer points and some signs of spirit spouses were taken from Evangelist Joshua Orekhie Ministries (www.evangelistjoshua.com).

PRACTICAL WAYS TO DETHRONE THE SPIRIT SPOUSE STRONGMAN

> ## Sacrificial Prayer + Fasting.

"Howbeit this kind goeth not out but by prayer and fasting."
– Matthew 17:21

> ## Consistent Praise + Worship.

It lets your spirit yield to God instead of the spirit spouse. Consistent praise and worship can break/remove the stronghold of demonic powers from your life and lift the influence of spirits from your life. Having a personal atmosphere of worship repels demonic spirits and their influence. Submit to God in worship, resist the devil, and he *will* flee.

> ## Binding the Strongman + Intense Consumption of Word Study/Meditation.

To begin removing the spirit spouse strongman from your life, we must consider the scripture **Matthew 3:27**, which says, *"No man can enter into a strongman's house, and spoil his goods, except he will first bind the strong man;*

and then he will spoil his house.". In the spirit, the spirit spouses' affliction of you takes residence in your body and mind (the actual stronghold/much of the influence is in the mind/soul). Your body/soul is where it resides or has a temporary residence.

It may not be apparent now, but as you follow through with deliverance, it will eventually manifest and make its presence known. So, to defeat it, we must first "bind" it. To bind is to *"tie or fasten (something) tightly together.".* This is done through declarations, using the Word, and even prophetic actions using your hands in a binding motion.

To effectively remove this stronghold, we must bind it (e.g., say, *"Spirit spouse, in the authority and power of Jesus Christ given to me, I bind you in the name of Jesus! I bind you here on earth and I declare that you are also bound in the heavens!).* After it is bound, you are now free to spoil its goods and whatever it has taken from you.

N.B: After binding any strongman/demonic spirit, and it leaves your body, the vacancy it left in you must be filled with something else!

What should replace it is the Word of God. When spirits are cast out of a person, they leave and wander. Then they may come back to see if the place they left is still available in you. If it is, whereas nothing has replaced the spirit's place (no acceptance of Christ, receiving of the Holy Spirit, no Word, etc.), then the spirit will come back with the company! This is why delivering an unrepentant person/unbeliever can be dangerous.

Reference: Matthew 12:43-45
"Now when the unclean spirit has gone out of a man, it roams through waterless (dry, arid) places in search of rest, but it does not find it. Then it says, 'I will return to my house from which I came.' And when it arrives, it finds the place unoccupied, swept, and put in order. Then it brings seven other spirits more wicked than itself, and they go in and make their home there. And the last condition of that man becomes worse than the first..."

So, it is particularly important that as you go through deliverance, at any stage, you consistently spend time in the Word of God. It will not only fill you, but as you read and meditate upon it, it will stick to your remembrance. Doing so makes prayer and warfare much easier, as you'll be better able to remember scripture, pray, and speak it over yourself! There is power in declaring the Word of God!

SCRIPTURES FOR DEFEATING SPIRIT SPOUSES

We must never forget that the weapons of our warfare are not carnal, and the Sword we use as Believers to fight is the Word of God. You can find any scripture that applies to your situation (ask the Holy Spirit for help on which ones would be best to use). Here are a few scriptures you can apply as you tear down this stronghold, reclaim your body and believe God for change:

> ➤ **1 Corinthians 3:16-17:** *"Do you not know that you are the temple of God and that the Spirit of God dwells in you? If anyone defiles the temple of God, God will destroy him. For the temple of God is holy, which temple you are."*

Prayer Example: Heavenly Father, I acknowledge that my body is your sacred temple. I affirm that only your Spirit should reside in this temple. This 'spirit spouse' and all its defiling influences, I call upon you to utterly destroy and remove from me! Your Word assures that anyone who defiles my temple, you will destroy. By your Word, I proclaim that you will eradicate this' spirit spouse' in the powerful name of Jesus!

> *Luke 10:19: "Behold, I give you the authority to trample on serpents and scorpions, and over all the power of the enemy, and nothing shall by any means hurt you."*

Prayer Example: Lord, I am grateful for the authority you've bestowed upon me. With this authority, I trample on serpents, scorpions, and all the powers of 'spirit spouses' in the name of Jesus! By your Word and power, I declare that nothing these' spirit spouses' do will harm me in any way, in the name of Jesus!

> *Romans 16:20: "And the God of peace will crush Satan under your feet shortly."*

Prayer Example: Lord, I thank you that the time has come for this spirit spouse to be crushed under my feet. Deliverance is my portion! The affliction of spirit spouses in my life has come to an end! I pray, oh God, of my peace, that you will crush this spirit spouse and anything that comes with it under my feet in the name of Jesus!

MANIFESTATIONS OF DELIVERANCE

When spirits begin to manifest and encounter the power of God during deliverance, there are ways to spot them. As you go through self-deliverance or observe deliverance elsewhere, these are some signs that testify to the presence of a demonic spirit/spirit spouse manifesting through a person:

- Screaming.
- Screeching.
- Gnashing of teeth.
- Irritated/Annoyed behavior, shaking and/or fidgeting.
- Vomiting.
- Belching/Burping.
- Yawning.
- Excessive/Evil laughter.
- Pretending to be asleep/Drowsiness.
- Pretending to be mute/dumb.
- Use of hands to block the person's ears, eyes, or wherever the deliverance minister may touch.
- Fighting/Violent behavior.

- Flatulating.

- Excretion (needing to use the bathroom).

- Sneezing.

- Frothing.

- Drooling.

- Spitting.

- Stretching

- Weakness/Lightness/Feeling tired

- Difficulty standing/concentrating/focusing

SIGNS OF DELIVERANCE FROM SPIRIT SPOUSES

- ✓ No strong, uncontrollable sexual/lustful desires or thoughts.
- ✓ Your body will feel light, pure, free, clean.
- ✓ Your mind will be at peace.
- ✓ Any body parts the spirit spouse interfered with will now feel free/clean.
- ✓ Your prayer life will increase.
- ✓ Your devotional life with God will increase.
- ✓ Your dream life will increase, and you will receive more revelations and clearer communication from God via dreams without confusion or defilement.
- ✓ No more sexual/lustful/unclean dreams. Your dreams will be more peaceful, cleaner & clearer.
- ✓ You have better control over your mind and emotions and will not easily give into any sexual/lustful thoughts.
- ✓ Mental, emotional, and spiritual clarity.
- ✓ You will be more affectionate and kinder toward the opposite sex/your partner.

Nykefah Nairne

- ✓ Your thoughts will be more peaceful toward the opposite sex/your partner.
- ✓ Your life's purpose will become clearer and things you do in pursuit of purpose will become easier.
- ✓ Frustration, confusion, and discouragement will be removed from you.
- ✓ You will experience an increase in peace and joy.
- ✓ The opposite sex will begin to pursue you again without hindrance, delay, or failure.
- ✓ Restoration of relationship/marriage.
- ✓ Relational/Marital peace and fruitfulness.
- ✓ Increase in blessings, favor, and good opportunities.

ACKNOWLEDGEMENTS

I'd like first to acknowledge the precious Holy Spirit, who has been the most superb orchestrator of my life. Thank you for your consistency in keeping me in God's will and for bringing me through my own deliverance. I appreciate your presence, work, and grace in helping others the way you've helped me.

ABOUT THE AUTHOR

Nykefah Nairne is an Award-winning Jamaican Author who has so far penned and published 19 books. One of her most recent publications, **"Breaking the Mental Stronghold of Spirit Spouses: Your Guide to Mental Breakthrough"** won a local Indie Author Award under the category, "Best Women Empowerment" book.

She is not just an avid reader and writer, but also the Founder and Global Director of the Krowned Queens Academy.

Breaking the Stronghold of Spirit Spouses

The KQA is a women's ministry geared towards restoring the hearts of women and girls back God through discipleship, community, love, the prophetic, preaching and teaching of the Word of God. Not only is Nykefah known for these, but she has also been featured in Jamaica's most prominent newspaper, "The Gleaner", for a viral video of her evangelizing and sharing her testimony on a local bus full of passengers back in 2019.

In all that she does, she seeks to bring glory to God and to advance His kingdom here on earth as it is in Heaven.

Nykefah Nairne

Made in the USA
Coppell, TX
20 October 2024

38965952R00036